GIVING *the* BEST *of* YOURSELF *to* YOUR SPOUSE

COUPLES DAILY DEVOTIONAL

Nigel & Anrick Smith

Giving the Best of Yourself to Your Spouse: Couples Daily Devotional

Trilogy Christian Publishers
A Wholly Owned Subsidary of Trinity Broadcasting Network
2442 Michelle Drive, Tustin, CA 92780

Manufactured in the United States of America

Trilogy Disclaimer: The views and content expressed in this book are those of the author and may not necessarily reflect the views and doctrine of Trilogy Christian Publishing or the Trinity Broadcasting Network.

10 9 8 7 6 5 4 3 2 1
Library of Congress Cataloging-in-Publication Data is available.

ISBN 978-1-63769-314-8
ISBN 978-1-63769-315-5 (eBook)

DEDICATION

My husband and I want to dedicate this marriage devotional first to our two grown children, Michael Weeks and Alexandria Smith. To both our parents for their examples of what a lasting, loving marriage looks like. To our dear brothers and sisters in Christ, Pastor Tylia, and Elder Marcelto Cooks for letting us know that it is ok to date each other even after the marriage. Thank you to our Founding Pastor and Founding First Lady, Pastor Coleman and Pastor Pat, for their examples of a godly marriage. We also like to thank our Lead Pastor and First Lady, Pastor Carlos and Lady Monica, for their example of a godly married couple.

TABLE OF CONTENTS

INTRODUCTION

God intended for marriage to be the most intimate, fulfilling relationship that two people can experience. His Word describes marriage as a man and woman uniting to become one flesh. It took years for my husband Nigel and I to fully grasp God's perfect plan for marriage. Now that we have a greater understanding, our goal is to share it with you...

We hope that you will be encouraged to read this devotional daily; prayerfully together that you will experience God's perfect plan for your marriage through practical everyday things that you do with your spouse. It will not happen all at once, but rest assured that it will happen for you. With patience and God on your side, you will have a better marriage.

DAY 1

Marriage: Two Becoming One

What is marriage?
To unite as husband and wife.

When a young man leaves the home of his parents, let it not be for any other reason but to unite with his wife, and the two become one flesh.

> "For this reason a man shall leave his father
> and mother and be joined to his wife, and
> the two shall become one flesh."
> — Ephesians 5:31

And Adam said:

> "This is now bone of my bones And flesh of my
> flesh; She shall be called Woman, Because she
> was taken out of Man."
> Therefore a man shall leave his father and
> mother and be joined to his wife, and they
> shall become one flesh.
> — Genesis 2:23–24

The exchange of rings in a marriage ceremony represents an endless circle. A woman or man who has a spouse is bound together by a covenant as long as that spouse lives. But if one of them passes, the other is free to marry. Therefore, the phrase in the marriage vows that states: To death do us part should not be taken lightly. Marriage is a covenant between the man and woman but also between God.

> For the woman who has a husband is bound by
> the law to *her* husband as long as he lives. But if
> the husband dies, she is released from the law
> of *her* husband.
>
> — Romans 7:2

Sexual relations or sexual intimacy is a very important part of the marriage covenant. Permanent abstaining from sex deprives the other partner of his or her natural right and may open the door for temptation. The only time sexual relations are not permitted is through consent from both partners to fast and pray. Sexual relations should resume to prevent temptation.

> Let the husband render to his wife the affec-
> tion due her, and likewise also the wife to her
> husband. The wife does not have authority
> over her own body, but the husband does. And
> likewise the husband does not have authority
> over his own body, but the wife does. Do not
> deprive one another except with consent for
> a time, that you may give yourselves to fast-
> ing and prayer; and come together again so

that Satan does not tempt you because of your lack of self-control.

— Corinthians 7:3–5

When seeking a companion, it should be looked upon as a covenant and an unbroken promise. Both parties should be ready to commit to becoming one. Marital counseling is recommended, even if the couple is not a Christian. Marriage counseling gives guidance for the marriage.

> Yet you say, "For what reason?"
>> Because the Lord has been witness
>> Between you and the wife of your youth,
>> With whom you have dealt treacherously;
>> Yet she is your companion
>> And your wife by covenant.
>> But did He not make them one,
>> Having a remnant of the Spirit?
>> And why one?
>> He seeks godly offspring.
>> Therefore take heed to your spirit,
>> And let none deal treacherously with the
> wife of his youth.

— Malachi 2:14–15

God designed marriage to be a beautiful union to be enjoyed between a man and a woman. Much like that of our relationship with Him.

Do you have a personal relationship with God? If yes, record what that looks like.

_____

_____

_____

_____

_____

_____

_____

_____

_____

_____

_____

_____

_____

_____

_____

_____

_____

_____

DAY 2
God's Virtuous Family

Virtuous: moral excellence and righteousness.

The definition of a family, according to Webster's, is parents and their children.[1]

The union of a man and woman in marriage marks the beginning of a virtuous family in the eyes of God.

> Therefore a man shall leave his father and
> mother and be joined to his wife, and they
> shall become one flesh.
>
> — Genesis 2:24

When the husband and the wife have a relationship with God, it's their responsibility to minister to the entire household. Ministering to the entire household enables the whole family to grow together in their relationship with Christ.

> And he took them the same hour of the night
> and washed *their* stripes. And immediately he
> and all his *family* were baptized. Now when he

---

[1] Anne Soukhanov H., Kaethe Ellis, Laurel Cook, and Howard Webbe, "Virtuous," In *Webster's II New Riverside University Dictionary* (Boston, MA: Riverside Publishing Co, 1988), 282.

had brought them into his house, he set food
before them; and he rejoiced, having believed
in God with all his household.

— Acts 16:33–34

In a virtuous family, the man is the head of the home, as
God is the head of his life. Love also plays an important role
in every family. This love in a virtuous family begins with a
husband's love for his wife and extends to their children.
That love should be the same love that God has for him.

Wives, submit to your own husbands, as to the
Lord.

— Ephesians 5:22

And you, fathers, do not provoke your children
to wrath, but bring them up in the training and
admonition of the Lord.

— Ephesians 6:4

one who rules his own house well, having his children in submission with all rever-
ence (for if a man does not know how to rule
his own house, how will he take care of the
church of God?);

— 1 Timothy 3:4–5

In a virtuous family, the wife works with her husband as
a team in everything. Her heart is not only open and full of
love for her family but also for everyone she encounters. Her
home is always in order, and her door is always open. She

teaches the children the love of God and is always there for them with open arms.

Who can find a virtuous wife? For her
worth *is* far above rubies.

The heart of her husband safely trusts her;
So he will have no lack of gain.

She does him good and not evil All the days
of her life.

She seeks wool and flax, And willingly
works with her hands.

She is like the merchant ships, She brings
her food from afar.

She also rises while it is yet night, And provides food for her household, And a portion
for her maidservants.

She considers a field and buys it; From her
profits she plants a vineyard.

She girds herself with strength, And
strengthens her arms.

She perceives that her merchandise *is* good,
And her lamp does not go out by night.

She stretches out her hands to the distaff,
And her hand holds the spindle.

She extends her hand to the poor, Yes, she
reaches out her hands to the needy.

She is not afraid of snow for her household
For all her household *is* clothed with scarlet.

She makes tapestry for herself; Her clothing *is* fine linen and purple.

Her husband is known in the gates, When
he sits among the elders of the land.

She makes linen garments and sells *them,*
And supplies sashes for the merchants.

Strength and honor *are* her clothing; She
shall rejoice in time to come.

She opens her mouth with wisdom, And on
her tongue *is* the law of kindness.

She watches over the ways of her household,
And does not eat the bread of idleness.

Her children rise up and call her blessed;
Her husband *also,* and he praises her:

"Many daughters have done well, But you
excel them all."

Charm *is* deceitful and beauty *is* passing,
But a woman *who* fears the LORD, she shall be
praised.

Give her of the fruit of her hands, And let
her own works praise her in the gates.

— Proverbs 31:10–31

And when she and her household were bap-
tized, she begged *us,* saying, "If you have judged
me to be faithful to the Lord, come to my
house and stay." So she persuaded us.

— Acts 16:15

And the LORD God said, "*It is* not good that
man should be alone; I will make him a helper
comparable to him."

— Genesis 2:18

The role that children play in a virtuous family is to hon-
or and obey their parents in everything, not sometimes or

when they feel like it. This is a command from God that comes with a promise.

> Children obey your parents in all that you do for this is right. "Honor your father and mother," which is the first commandment with a promise. "That it may be well with you and you may live a long life."
>
> — Ephesians 6:1-3

Proverbs 22:6 tells us that when parents train up their children in the way they should go, they will not depart from it—the way of the Lord and His teachings.

With the husband and wife submitting to each other and serving God, the children honoring and obeying, we see God's plan for the virtuous family.

$\partial\!\!\!/\!\!\!\!\diagup$

_____

_____

_____

_____

_____

_____

_____

_____

GIVING *the* BEST *of* YOURSELF *to* YOUR SPOUSE

DAY 3

The Importance of Family

Family: parents and their children— relatives.

Whichever way you look at it, family is important to God. No family is perfect. We all have our issues, dysfunctional in some way or the other; family brings togetherness, joy, and happiness. God allowed Adam to name all the animals with hopes that he would find the joy of having the animals around him as family. However, Adam did not find joy in spending all his time with the animals he had named. He needed human interaction, someone with whom he could start a family.

> So God created man in His own image; in the image of God He created him; male and female He created them. Then God blessed them, and God said to them, "Be fruitful and multiply; fill the earth and subdue it; have dominion over the fish of the sea, over the birds of the air, and over every living thing that moves on the earth."
>
> — Genesis 1:27–28

And the LORD God said, "It is not good that man should be alone; I will make him a helper comparable to him." Out of the ground the LORD God formed every beast of the field and every bird of the air, and brought them to Adam to see what he would call them. And whatever Adam called each living creature, that was its name. So Adam gave names to all cattle, to the birds of the air, and to every beast of the field. But for Adam there was not found a helper comparable to him. And the LORD God caused a deep sleep to fall on Adam, and he slept; and He took one of his ribs, and closed up the flesh in its place. Then the rib which the LORD God had taken from man He made into a woman, and He brought her to the man.

— Genesis 2:18–23

We also see this importance of the family dynamic when God had Noah build an ark/boat to save his family from the flood that was coming upon on the earth. The boat served in saving Noah and his family as well as the animal species, two of every kind.

But I will establish My covenant with you; and you shall go into the ark—you, your sons, your wife, and your sons' wives with you.

— Genesis 6:18

What does it mean to be part of a family?

It means that we stick together, we support each other, and we comfort each other. But most importantly, to be part of a family means that we love each other no matter what. We see this in the story of Ruth and Naomie, where after Naomi had lost her sons and her husband and the family lineage was left up to her and her former daughter-in-law Ruth.

Now they took wives of the women of Moab: the name of the one was Orpah, and the name of the other Ruth. And they dwelt there about ten years. Then both Mahlon and Chilion also died; so the woman survived her two sons and her husband.

Then she arose with her daughters-in-law that she might return from the country of Moab, for she had heard in the country of Moab that the Lord had visited His people by giving them bread. Therefore she went out from the place where she was, and her two daughters-in-law with her; and they went on the way to return to the land of Judah. And Naomi said to her two daughters-in-law, "Go, return each to her mother's house. The Lord deal kindly with you, as you have dealt with the dead and with me. The Lord grant that you may find rest, each in the house of her husband."

So she kissed them, and they lifted up their voices and wept. And they said to her, "Surely we will return with you to your people."

But Naomi said, "Turn back, my daughters; why will you go with me? Are there still sons in my womb, that they may be your husbands? Turn back, my daughters, go—for I am too old to have a husband. If I should say I have hope, if I should have a husband tonight and should also bear sons, would you wait for them till they were grown? Would you restrain yourselves from having husbands? No, my daughters; for it grieves me very much for your sakes that the hand of the Lord has gone out against me!"

Then they lifted up their voices and wept again; and Orpah kissed her mother-in-law, but Ruth clung to her.

And she said, "Look, your sister-in-law has gone back to her people and to her gods; return after your sister-in-law."

But Ruth said: "Entreat me not to leave you, Or to turn back from following after you; For wherever you go, I will go; And wherever you lodge, I will lodge; Your people shall be my people, And your God, my God. Where you die, I will die, And there will I be buried. The Lord do so to me, and more also, If anything but death parts you and me."

When she saw that she was determined to go with her, she stopped speaking to her.

— Ruth 1:4–18

A family does not hold grievances against each other. We must be willing to forgive each other no matter what, as God has forgiven us. A great example of forgiveness in a family is Joseph and his brothers, after they put him in a pit and sold him into slavery. And yet Joseph found it in his heart to forgive them; it was not easy, of course, but he did it!

> Then they said to one another, "Look, this dreamer is coming! Come therefore, let us now kill him and cast him into some pit; and we shall say, 'Some wild beast has devoured him.' We shall see what will become of his dreams!" But Reuben heard it, and he delivered him out of their hands, and said, "Let us not kill him." And Reuben said to them, "Shed no blood, but cast him into this pit which is in the wilderness, and do not lay a hand on him"- that he might deliver him out of their hands, and bring him back to his father.
>
> So it came to pass, when Joseph had come to his brothers, that they stripped Joseph of his tunic, the tunic of many colors that was on him. Then they took him and cast him into a pit. And the pit was empty; there was no water in it. And they sat down to eat a meal. Then they lifted their eyes and looked, and there was a company of Ishmaelites, coming from Gilead with their camels, bearing spices, balm, and myrrh, on their way to carry them down to Egypt. So Judah said to his brothers, "What profit is there if we kill our brother and conceal his blood? Come and let us sell him to the Ishmaelites, and let not our hand be upon him, for he is our brother and our flesh." And

his brothers listened. Then Midianite traders passed by; so the brothers pulled Joseph up and lifted him out of the pit, and sold him to the Ishmaelites for twenty shekels of silver. And they took Joseph to Egypt.

— Genesis 37:19–28

And Joseph said to his brothers, "Please come near to me." So they came near. Then he said: "I am Joseph your brother, whom you sold into Egypt. But now, do not therefore be grieved or angry with yourselves because you sold me here; for God sent me before you to preserve life. For these two years the famine has been in the land, and there are still five years in which there will be neither plowing nor harvesting. And God sent me before you to preserve a posterity for you in the earth, and to save your lives by a great deliverance. So now it was not you who sent me here, but God; and He has made me a father to Pharaoh, and lord of all his house, and a ruler throughout all the land of Egypt."

Then he fell on his brother Benjamin's neck and wept, and Benjamin wept on his neck.

— Genesis 45:4–8, 14

Let's always take the time to appreciate our family!

DAY 4

The Power in Forgiveness

Forgiveness: to pardon
or bring freedom

Forgiveness is rooted in love. Remember when Jesus was on the cross, He said, "Father forgive them, for they do not know what they do" (Luke 23:34). He said this as the soldiers were casting lots on His clothes, dividing them up amongst themselves. As they did all this, Jesus asked the Father to forgive them. If we love each other, we should be willing to forgive each other no matter the issue. We cannot expect forgiveness from God if we are not willing to forgive others.

> And forgive us our debts, As we forgive our debtors.
>
> — Matthew 6:12

> "Judge not, and you shall not be judged. Condemn not, and you shall not be condemned. Forgive, and you will be forgiven."
>
> — Luke 6:37

> bearing with one another, and forgiving one
> another, if anyone has a complaint against
> another; even as Christ forgave you, so you
> also must do.
>
> — Colossians 3:13

You see, 1 John 4:18 tells us that there is no fear in love and that the perfect love of God drives out all fear. If the love of God lives in us because the Spirit of God lives in us, we should have no fear of forgiving someone that has hurt us because the fear is not of God.

First Peter 4:8 tells us to keep on loving each other because God's perfect love covers all our sins. So, no matter how much someone has wronged you or hurt you, let your love, the love of God that is in you, cover them and bring them to forgiveness. Forgiveness also brings closure for the person that did the wrong as well as the person that was wronged. Forgiveness allows you to have peace even if the person that has wronged you does not accept the gift of forgiveness.

If we are not willing to forgive others, how can we then expect our heavenly Father to forgive us?

> "For if you forgive men their trespasses, your
> heavenly Father will also forgive you. But if you
> do not forgive men their trespasses, neither
> will your Father forgive your trespasses.
>
> — Matthew 6:14–15

And be kind to one another, tenderhearted, forgiving one another, even as God in Christ forgave you.

— Ephesians 4:32

Forgiving is for you more than the person who has done the offense. Forgiveness frees you from the guilt, hurt, pain, and whatever else may be associated with it.

_____

_____

_____

_____

_____

_____

_____

_____

_____

_____

_____

_____

_____

_____

GIVING *the* BEST *of* YOURSELF *to* YOUR SPOUSE

DAY 5

Responsibility as Parents

Responsibility: involving the ability
or authority to act on one's own—
reliable, accountability, answerable.

Psalm 127:3 tells us that children are an "...heritage from the Lord, The fruit of the womb is a reward."

As parents, God has given us the charge and responsibility to train up our children in His Word.

Proverbs 22:6 tells us to "train up a child in the way he should go, And when he is old he will not depart from it." Our children will not always do as we tell them, but if we train them up in the wisdom of the Lord, we don't have to worry because He will bring them back to Himself.

Children are to honor their parents as this is the first commitment with a promise. But it's also the parent's responsibility to discipline them correctly and not provoke them or anger them to do wrong.

Ephesians 6:1–4 talks about discipline as a form of correction, not punishment as the world would have us to view it. The rod of correction imparts wisdom to our children. The rod of correction is to be done with love, not anger.

Proverbs 29:15, when we train our children up according to the Word of God, we are imparting wisdom and hope for their future.

Proverbs 13:24, a man who loves his children is careful to discipline them, but a man who doesn't discipline his children does not love them.

> When we take our responsibility as parents seriously to train, teach, and discipline our children, the foundation that has been set in their lives by the Word of God will secure their lives and future for generations to come. They will one day take care of us and pass on the same teaching and training to their children. Now *for* the third time I am ready to come to you. And I will not be burdensome to you; for I do not seek yours, but you. For the children ought not to lay up for the parents, but the parents for the children.
>
> — 2 Corinthians 12:14

DAY 6

The Power of Prayer

What is prayer?
Prayer gives us strength.
We gain authority, victory,
and strength when we pray.

The meaning of prayer is the act of praying to God or a set of words addressed to God.[2]

Prayer is a powerful gift given to us by God to communicate with Him but also to move the forces of the enemy. The Bible tells us that God has given us the power to trample over the enemy.

> Behold, I give you the authority to trample on serpents and scorpions, and over all the power of the enemy, and nothing shall by any means hurt you.
>
> — Luke 10:19

Another verse of scripture tells us that we have also been given the power to call things that are not as though they are. And yet, another scripture tells us that he has given us

[2] Anne H. Soukhanov, Kaethe Ellis, Laurel Cook, and Howard Webber, "Prayer," In *Webster's II New Riverside University Dictionary* (Boston, MA: Riverside Publishing Co., 1988), 616.

the power to lose and bind things both in heaven and in the earth.

> "Assuredly, I say to you, whatever you bind on
> earth will be bound in heaven, and whatever
> you loose on earth will be loosed in heaven."
> — Matthew 18:18

All this power comes through prayer.

As important as prayer is, it is even more important for husbands and wives to pray together. The Bible tells us "that if two of you shall agree on earth as touching any thing that they shall ask, it shall be done for them of my Father which is in heaven" (Matthew 18:19). Touching and agreeing are done through prayer. We can move mountains when we pray. Imagine the power of prayer when it's done together in marriage!

Author Stormie Omaritian states in her book, *"The Power of a Praying Wife,"* that God taught her how to daily lay down her life in prayer for her husband, Michael.[3] I am sure this was not easy for her to do. But she denied herself and prayed for her husband daily. She also goes on to say that " a wife's prayers for her husband have a far greater effect on him than anyone else, even his mother."[4] This is the power that is experienced when spouses pray for each other!

Prayer is power, and prayer is a weapon!

---

[3] Stormie Omartian, *The Power of a Praying Wife*, (Eugene, OR: Harvest House Publishers, 2014).
[4] Omartian, *The Power of a Praying Wife*.

GIVING *the* BEST *of* YOURSELF *to* YOUR SPOUSE

DAY 7

Praying the Word of God

The Bible promises that when we lift our petitions to Him, He hears us. God's ears are inclined to hear, listen, and answer our prayers.

> The eyes of the Lord are on the righteous, And
> His ears are open to their cry.
>
> — Psalm 34:15

Therefore, it is important to pray according to the will of God. How do we know the will of God, you may ask? The will of God is found in reading His Word. Thus, praying the Word is also important. Jesus taught His disciples how to pray the will of God and the Word of God in *The Lord's Prayer*:

> "… Our father who in heaven,
> Hallowed be Your name,
> Your kingdom come
> Your will be done
> On earth as it is in heaven…"
>
> — Matthew 6:9–13

When we pray the Word of God or according to His will, we are magnifying His Word over our problems. We are exalting His Word. We are told in Scripture that God holds His Word above His name.

> ...For You have magnified Your word above all
> Your name.
>
> — Psalm 138:2b

When we pray the Word of God, we're putting Him in remembrance of His Word, and promises.

Praying the Word of God will bring life to our dead situations; no matter what they may be, God can cause life to come back again.

> Again He said to me, "Prophesy to these bones,
> and say to them, 'O dry bones, hear the word
> of the Lord! Thus says the Lord God to these
> bones: "Surely I will cause breath to enter into
> you, and you shall live.
>
> — Ezekiel 37:4–5

Ezekiel spoke life to some dead dried up old bones, but he did not do it by just saying anything that came to his mind. No he spoke the Word of God, and wouldn't you know it, flesh began to come onto those dead bones and then life—that which was dead was now a living breathing being. We show faith when we pray the Word of God—Faith in Him and His Word. We show that we trust Him and His Word. Jesus says His Word will not come back void but will accomplish that which He sends it out to do.

So shall My word be that goes forth from
My mouth; It shall not return to Me void,
But it shall accomplish what I please, And it
shall prosper in the thing for which I sent it.

— Isaiah 55:11

_____

_____

_____

_____

_____

_____

_____

_____

_____

_____

_____

_____

_____

_____

_____

GIVING *the* BEST *of* YOURSELF *to* YOUR SPOUSE

DAY 8

The Sustaining Power of God

The word sustain means to maintain or supply with the necessities, to keep up, support.[5]

We always need the sustaining power of God in our lives, in our homes, marriages, place of work, and every situation we face.

God has promised that He will never leave us or forsake us.

> Let your conduct be without covetous-
> ness; be content with such things as you have.
> For He Himself has said, "I will never leave you
> nor forsake you."
> — Hebrews 13:5

> He also tells us to cast all our cares and bur-
> dens on him because he cares for us. "Casting
> all your care upon him; for he careth for you."
> — I Peter 5:7

As people, we like to bear the weight of things all by our-selves. But God tells us that if we give Him our burdens, He

---

[5] "Sustain," Merriam-Webster Online Dictionary (Merriam-Webster, Incorporated, 2021), https://www.merriam-webster.com/dictionary/sustain.

will not only carry them for us, but He will keep us while He carries them. God doesn't want us to be burdened with the cares and concerns of this world.

> Even to your old age, I am He, And even to gray hairs I will carry you! I have made, and I will bear; Even I will carry, and will deliver you.
>
> — Isaiah 46:4

> Cast your burden on the Lord, And He shall sustain you; He shall never permit the righteous to be moved.
>
> — Psalms 55:22

We are told not to be conformed to this world but to be transformed through the renewing of our minds, through the Word of God daily.

When we cannot stand because of the cares of this world, God has promised to strengthen us.

> He gives power to the weak, And to those who have no might He increases strength. Even the youths shall faint and be weary, And the young men shall utterly fall, But those who wait on the Lord Shall renew their strength; They shall mount up with wings like eagles, They shall run and not be weary, They shall walk and not faint.
>
> — Isaiah 40:29–31

He keeps us not by His power or His might but by His Spirit, His Holy presence.

> So he answered and said to me: "This is the word of the Lord to Zerubbabel: 'Not by might nor by power, but by My Spirit,' Says the Lord of hosts.
>
> — Zechariah 4:6

We can't see or feel Him, but we know that He is present. God has always promised to keep us, strengthen us, deliver us, protect us, and so much more as long as we allow Him to.

$\ll$

_____

_____

_____

_____

_____

_____

_____

_____

_____

_____

_____

GIVING *the* BEST *of* YOURSELF *to* YOUR SPOUSE

DAY 9

Compassion

Compassion: sorrow or pity
caused by the suffering
or misfortune of another.[6]

Simply put, compassion is showing love for all. God had compassion on us when He sent His only son to die for us.

> For God so loved the world that He gave His
> only begotten Son, that whoever believes in
> Him should not perish but have everlasting
> life.
>
> —John 3:16

He also shows us compassion daily through His grace. Scripture tells us that:

> It is of the Lord's mercies that we are not con-
> sumed because his compassions fail not. They
> are new every morning…
>
> — Lamentations 3:22–23 KJV

---

[6] "Compassion," In *Merriam-Webster Intermediate Dictionary* (Springfield, MA: Merriam-Webster Incorporated, 2016), 154.

Compassion is a characteristic of God. It is who He is. If we say we want to be like Jesus, then we must show the same compassion. This must become a part of our character, too.

> Therefore, as *the* elect of God, holy and beloved, put on tender mercies, kindness, humility, meekness, longsuffering;
> — Colossians 3:12

> "But the fruit of the spirit is love, joy, peace, longsuffering, kindness, goodness, faithfulness, gentleness, self-control. Against such there is no law."
> — Galatians 5:22–23

I once heard Joyce Myer say in one of her teachings that the fruit of the spirit "has two bookends which begins with love and ends with faithfulness holding everything else in its place."[7] You see, you cannot go wrong with showing love. It sums up Christianity; it is the whole basis of Christianity.

Jesus' compassion for us drives Him to care for us in so many ways. He provides for us; He heals our bodies when we are sick and so much more. He does not always give us what we want but what He knows we need. God will always have compassion on us regardless of what we have done. He will always forgive us; that is His character. We see this illustrated in the prodigal son, the wasteful son, yet God had compassion on him.

---

[7] "Joyce Meyer Ministries - Enjoying Everyday Life TV Show" (Joyce Meyer Ministries, 2021), https://joycemeyer.org/todaysshow.

"And he arose and came to his father. But when he was still a great way off, his father saw him and had compassion, and ran and fell on his neck and kissed him. And the son said to him, 'Father, I have sinned against heaven and in your sight, and am no longer worthy to be called your son.'"

"But the father said to his servants, 'Bring out the best robe and put it on him, and put a ring on his hand and sandals on his feet. And bring the fatted calf here and kill it, and let us eat and be merry; for this my son was dead and is alive again; he was lost and is found.'" And they began to be merry.

— Luke 15:20–24

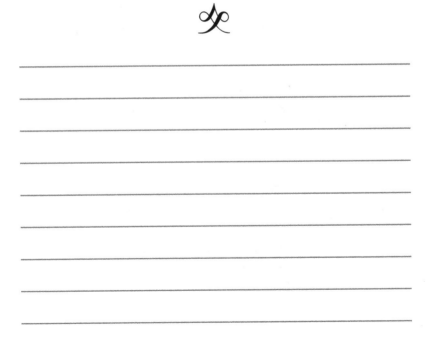

GIVING *the* BEST *of* YOURSELF *to* YOUR SPOUSE

DAY 10

Stewardship

S tewardship is a big part of marriage, as well as our relationship with God. To be a steward means to head, rule,
oversee, and manage—one who manages another's property
or affairs. A steward is one who is trustworthy.[8]

Trust in marriage is part of being a steward, trust between both the husband and wife. The wife trusts the husband, and the husband trusts the wife. This trust stems in
many forms such as... Trust in the finances, the management
of the household, and trust to be honorable to each other.

Jesus also calls us to be stewards over His finances and
affairs of the kingdom. Malachi 3:8–12 tells us to bring all
the tithes into the storehouse of God, and then it says to test
Him in our obedience to see if He will bless us. Stewardship
leads to blessings. You see, a steward is a servant of God.
Someone that God has entrusted with the secret things of
the kingdom.

> Let a man so consider us, as servants of
> Christ and stewards of the mysteries of God.
> — 1 Corinthians 4:1

---

[8] "Steward," In *Merriam-Webster Intermediate Dictionary* (Springfield, MA: Merriam-Webster Incorporated, 2016), 787.

As good stewards, we should always be prepared to do what God calls us to do. We should be obedient to the will of God. The life of a steward is lived out by using Godly wisdom and making the right decisions. A good steward supervises and takes good care of the things that God has given them—stewardship. Hence, in being obedient to God through good stewardship, just like trust in a marital relationship is earned, we show ourselves faithful to God and then we are trustworthy to receive the blessings of His gifts.

_____

_____

_____

_____

_____

_____

_____

_____

_____

_____

_____

_____

DAY 11

The Name of Jesus

When we think about a name, for instance, when naming our children, do we think about its meaning?

A name is to call, to say, to appeal.

A name has power. A name has dominion. A name has or gives authority to the one bearing that name. For example, when you hear the name of Jesus that was given to Him by His heavenly father and not His earthly mother, Mary. What do you think of when you hear the name of Jesus? I do not know about You, but I think about love, power, authority, and my elder brother. The name of Jesus says who He is, mighty, powerful, and a spiritual force.

> Therefore God also has highly exalted Him
> and given Him the name which is above ev-
> ery name, that at the name of Jesus every
> knee should bow, of those in heaven, and
> of those on earth, and of those under the
> earth, and that every tongue should confess
> that Jesus Christ is Lord, to the glory of God
> the Father.
>
> — Philippians 2:9–11

The name of Jesus is so powerful that demons tremble at the very mention of His name. The name of Jesus is so powerful not only will demons tremble, but every knee will bow, and every tongue will confess His name that He is Lord.

> For it is written:
> "As I live, says the Lord,
> Every knee shall bow to Me,
> And every tongue shall confess to God."
>
> — Romans 14:11

The name of Jesus has the power to transform the lives and hearts of everyone who calls upon Him. When we call on the name of Jesus, the name above all other names both in heaven and on earth, He hears us, He answers us, stands to protect us, and provides for us. The name of Jesus!

_____

_____

_____

_____

_____

_____

_____

_____

DAY 12

To Know Him

Let us look at the definition of the word *know*: To understand, to have knowledge of. To be acquainted with.[9]

To know Jesus is to understand who He is, have knowledge of who He is, and become acquainted with Him. How do we do this, you may ask? It is quite easy; you must have a relationship with Him—and repent of our sins and welcome Him into our hearts and lives. Knowing Jesus is to have a heartfelt relationship with Him.

> Then I will give them a heart to know Me, that
> I am the Lord; and they shall be My people,
> and I will be their God, for they shall return to
> Me with their whole heart.
> —Jeremiah 24:7

He is the creator of the universe, and we belong to Him in every way.

---

[9] "Know," In *Merriam-Webster Intermediate Dictionary* (Springfield, MA: Merriam-Webster Incorporated, 2016), 433.

Know that the Lord, He is God; it
is He who has made us, and not we ourselves;
we are His people and the sheep of His pasture.
— Psalm 100:3

Knowing God is knowing that He is our shepherd that watches over us, His sheep. He promises that He will never leave us or forsake us. A relationship with God involves knowing His resurrection power. We were all once dead in our sins, but His resurrection power brought us all to life in Him.

Therefore we were buried with Him through
baptism into death, that just as Christ was
raised from the dead by the glory of the Father, even so we also should walk in newness of
life.
— Romans 6:4

On this Christian journey, there will be times when God tells us to be still and know that He is God.

Be still, and know that I am God;
I will be exalted among the nations,
I will be exalted in the earth!
— Psalm 46:10

The only way we can be still is to have a relationship with Him and have had experience with Him. Not knowing, not having a relationship with God is a dangerous place to be. We must take time to know Him, and build a loving, life-changing relationship with the Father and creator of the universe. Unless we let Jesus in we, will not have any part with Him.

> Peter said to Him, "You shall never wash my feet!"
> Jesus answered him, "If I do not wash you, you have no part with Me."
> — John 13:8

He will say at the end of time part from me I never knew you.

> But he answered and said, 'Assuredly, I say to you, I do not know you.'
> — Matthew 25:12

_____

_____

_____

_____

_____

_____

_____

_____

GIVING *the* BEST *of* YOURSELF *to* YOUR SPOUSE

DAY 13

Salvation: Restoration

Salvation: in Christianity,
deliverance or redemption is the
saving of human beings from death
and separation from God by Christ's
death and resurrection.

Restoration: an act of restoring or the
condition of being restored.[10]

When we think of these two strong and profound words, *salvation* and *restoration*, what comes to your mind? Two things stick out for me. One is *newness*. God has made all things new in my life through restoration. He has restored my life and will restore yours as well. Second, all my sins are washed away, free from the death of my past sins. Amen and Hallelujah to the Lamb!

When we accept Christ into our lives as our savior, He restores us back to Himself.

---

[10] "Restoration," In *Merriam-Webster Intermediate Dictionary* (Springfield, MA: Merriam-Webster Incorporated, 2016), 674.

Restore us, O God;
Cause Your face to shine,
And we shall be saved!

— Psalm 80:3

When we accept Christ as our Lord and savior, there is a certain joy that comes over us. Scripture calls this joy un-speakable joy, joy without words.

Whom having not seen, ye love; in whom,
though now ye see him not, yet believing, ye
rejoice with joy unspeakable and full of glory.

— I Peter 1:8 KJV

That joy is God restoring us from the person we once were into a new creation.

Restore to me the joy of Your salvation,
And uphold me by Your generous Spirit.

— Psalm 51:12

If any man be is in Christ, he is a new creation;
old things have passed away; behold all things
have become new.

— 2 Corinthians 5:17

Before any of us came to know and accept Christ as our savior, we were bound by certain things of life (things of the devil, enemy). Then once we accepted Christ, freed us from those things that held us bound. He took off those grave clothes so that we can be free in and through Him.

Now when He had said these things, He
cried with a loud voice, "Lazarus, come
forth!" And he who had died came out bound
hand and foot with graveclothes, and his
face was wrapped with a cloth. Jesus said to
them, "Loose him, and let him go."

—John 11:43–44

Lazarus was bound by death and grave clothes, but Jesus told the people to lose him and set him free because he was no longer bound but alive and free. This is the life we were meant to live, one of joy, peace, love, and freedom from sin, death, and the grave. Even death in Christ, we still live, we still are victorious,

"Where O death where is your victory? Where
O death where is your sting?"

— 1 Corinthians 15:55 NIV

Don't be bound by your past but be freed by your future.

GIVING *the* BEST *of* YOURSELF *to* YOUR SPOUSE

DAY 14

Salvation: The Love of God

For God so loved the word that he gave his one
and only Son, that whoever believes in him
shall not perish but have eternal life.

— John 3:16 NIV

This is probably one of the most known scripture in the
Bible by Christians and non-Christians alike. But do
we truly know what the love of God is? Have you really experienced the love of the Father? What is love?

Scripture tells us that love is patient, love is kind, and it
is not boastful.

Love suffers long and is kind; love does not
envy; love does not parade itself, is not puffed
up;

— 1 Corinthians 13:4

Love: "is an inner quality expressed
outwardly as a commitment to seek
the well-being of others through

concrete acts of service."[11]

Wow! You mean this is what Jesus did for us? He gave up His life for us, not for His well-being but ours so that we might have a life-changing relationship with Him. That is *love!*

It was love that kept Jesus nailed to the cross; it was not the nails. His love for humankind. Though we did not know him or cared to know Him, he sacrificed His life for ours.

> But God demonstrates His own love toward us, in that while we were still sinners, Christ died for us.
>
> — Romans 5:8

> In this the love of God was manifested toward us, that God has sent His only begotten Son into the world, that we might live through Him. In this is love, not that we loved God, but that He loved us and sent His Son to be the propitiation for our sins.
>
> — 1 John 4:9–10

> Greater love has no one than this, than to lay down one's life for his friends.
>
> — John 15:13

His love brought us salvation, a relationship with Him like no other. Salvation gives us a new life, a new beginning. Nothing or no one can separate us from the love of God. God loves us so much that no matter what the trouble, the

11 "Love: NCCG.ORG" (The Messianic Evangelicals, 2018), http://nccg.org/love.html.

situation, He still loves us and will always be there for us. We do not have to be perfect in our walk with Him; He just asks for our best effort to live a life that is pleasing in His sight.

> Who shall separate us from the love of Christ? Shall tribulation, or distress, or persecution, or famine, or nakedness, or peril, or sword? As it is written:
>
> "For Your sake we are killed all day long. We are accounted as sheep for the slaughter."
>
> Yet in all these things we are more than conquerors through Him who loved us. For I am persuaded that neither death nor life, nor angels nor principalities nor powers, nor things present nor things to come, nor height nor depth, nor any other created thing, shall be able to separate us from the love of God which is in Christ Jesus our Lord.
>
> — Romans 8:35–39

_____

_____

_____

_____

_____

_____

GIVING *the* BEST *of* YOURSELF *to* YOUR SPOUSE

DAY 15

Faith: What Is It?

Merriam-Webster's Dictionary tells us that one of the definitions of *faith* is the "firm belief" even in the absences of proof.[12] In comparison, the New Strong's Complete Dictionary of Bible Words tells us one of its definitions of *faith* is an "expectation; hope."[13]

All these definitions sound well and good, but the Word of God says it best in Hebrews 11:1 (NIV):

> Now faith is the confidence in what we hope
> for and assurance about what we do not see.

That is by far my favorite definition. This is my personal definition of faith: It is our firsthand experiences with God, seeing Him move in our lives, even when we don't see Him moving, we trust and believe that He is working everything out for our good and His glory.

---

[12] "Faith," Merriam-Webster Online Dictionary (Merriam-Webster, Incorporated, 2021), https://www.merriam-webster.com/dictionary/faith.

[13] James Strong, *The New Strong's Complete Dictionary of Bible Words*. (Nelson Word Publishing Group, 1996), 93.

And we know that in all things God works for
the good of those who love him, who have been
called according to his purpose.
                                    — Romans 8:28 NIV

In order to have faith in God, first, we must believe in
Him. Then we must be taught the Word of God, and as we
are taught, our faith grows and develops through our life
experiences with God.

So then faith comes by hearing, and hearing by
the word of God.
                                    — Romans 10:17

You see, without faith, it is impossible to please God.
This means that if we do not believe in Him then we cannot please Him. How can you please someone you do not
love, much less believe in? It is just like trying to please
your spouse when the love has diminished. It is hard, at that
point, you are just going through the motions of love.

But without faith it is impossible to
please Him, for he who comes to God must
believe that He is, and that He is a rewarder of
those who diligently seek Him.
                                    — Hebrews 11:6

Our faith never starts out big; nothing does. The Bible
talks about a mustard seed faith. Imagine a mustard seed. It
is said to be one of the smallest seeds; you can barely see it.
But this is how the Bible said we start out on our faith jour-

ney (walk), and as we experience God moving in our lives, our faith grows from a mustard seed to great faith—Faith that can move mountains, but even mustard seed faith can move mountains.

> So Jesus said to them, "Because of your unbe-
> lief; for assuredly, I say to you, if you have faith
> as a mustard seed, you will say to this moun-
> tain, 'Move from here to there,' and it will
> move; and nothing will be impossible for you.
> — Matthew 17:20

Many times we tend to focus on the mountains in our lives and not on the mountain mover—God. God wants us to keep our eyes on Him. You see, our faith begins and ends with Him. Scripture tells us that He is the author and fin- isher (perfector) of our faith. In other words, He is at the beginning and the end of our faith.

> looking unto Jesus, the author and finisher
> of *our* faith, who for the joy that was set before
> Him endured the cross, despising the shame,
> and has sat down at the right hand of the
> throne of God.
> — Hebrews 12:2

GIVING *the* BEST *of* YOURSELF *to* YOUR SPOUSE

DAY 16

Putting Your Trust in God: What Does That Look Like?

Proverbs 3:5–6 tells us to "trust in the Lord and lean not on your own understanding" (NIV). "In all your ways acknowledge Him, And He will make your paths straight" (NASB). This means that no matter how bad things seem, you can believe God. Many times, our understanding or lack thereof will cause us not to trust God. Acknowledge His teaching, His guiding Holy Spirit, His Word. God is always talking but are we truly listening? As we write this section, would you believe this is exactly where we are right now?. God is funny like that. I know He's telling us to trust Him and not fear or worry.

When we decide to put our trust in God, we should trust Him with our whole heart. When we do this, we are not relying on ourselves or anyone else but God. When we put our trust in people and not God, we are setting ourselves up for disappointment and failure. You see, when we put our complete trust in God, we will never be disappointed. We set ourselves up for the blessing of God to flow in and through our lives.

"Blessed is the man who trusts in the Lord
And whose hope is the Lord.
For he shall be like a tree planted by the waters,
Which spreads out its roots by the river,
And will not]fear when heat comes;
But its leaf will be green,
And will not be anxious in the year of drought,
Nor will cease from yielding fruit."

—Jerimiah 17:7–8

God is the one person we always need to trust, not some of the time or with somethings. God says to trust Him at all times in and with all things.

Trust in Him at all times, you people;
Pour out your heart before Him;
God is a refuge for us. Selah.

— Psalm 62:8

What does it look like to trust in God? Trusting in God brings us joy, peace, hope, and blessings no matter the circumstance or situations we may face in life.

And God is able to make all grace abound toward you, that you, always having all sufficiency in all things, may have an abundance for every good work.

— 2 Corinthians 9:8

Trusting in God gives us protection from the enemy; it gives us strength when we are week.

I will say of the Lord, "He is my refuge and my fortress; My God, in Him I will trust."

— Psalm 91:2

Trust: To be firm, faithful, true: to trust—To be confident or sure, firm reliance: confident belief.[14] The condition of having confidence placed in one responsibility—future hope.

_____

_____
_____
_____
_____
_____
_____
_____
_____
_____
_____
_____
_____

[14] "Trust," In *Merriam-Webster Intermediate Dictionary* (Springfield, MA: Merriam-Webster Incorporated, 2016), 863.

GIVING *the* BEST *of* YOURSELF *to* YOUR SPOUSE

DAY 17

Trusting in God Part Two

There is never a good time to give up on anything, especially on God. Just at the moment you give up and call it quits, your blessing was waiting for you around the next corner. I saw this quote, and I liked it... "Keep going, everything you need will come to you at the right time."[15] Trusting God is never giving up on Him, His promises, or your dreams.

The promises of God are yea/yes and amen.

> For all the promises of God in Him are Yes,
> and in Him Amen, to the glory of God through
> us.
> — 2 Corinthians 1:20

This means whatever He says in His Word, He will do for you. All we have to do is trust Him.

Trusting God first begins with a relationship with Him. Trusting God comes from not only having a relationship with Him, but trusting Him brings peace; trusting Him brings rest. Psalm 9:10 says, "Those who know your name trust in you..."

---

[15] "Quote by Anonymous" Quotespedia (2021), https://www.quotespedia.org/authors/a/anonymous/keep-going-everything-you-need-will-come-to-you-at-the-perfect-time-anonymous/.

When we trust in God, we are also trusting in His love. His love says He will never leave us or forsake us. This love causes us to rejoice in Him.

> But I have trusted in Your mercy;
> My heart shall rejoice in Your salvation.
> — Psalm 13:5

Yes, it is a choice when we want to place our trust in God. He said we will be like mount Zion, which cannot be moved or shaken no matter what.

> Those who trust in the Lord
> Are like Mount Zion,
> Which cannot be moved, but abides forever.
> — Psalm 125:1

We must choose to trust and stand firm.

If we put our trust in ourselves or someone else, God says we are fools. But if we put our trust in Him, we will not be moved; we will prosper.

> He who is of a proud heart stirs up strife, but
> he who trusts in the Lord will be prospered. He
> who trusts in his own heart is a fool, but who-
> ever walks wisely will be delivered.
> — Proverbs 28:25–26

Those who trust in Him, will be kept in perfect peace.

You will keep him in perfect peace,
whose mind is stayed on You, because he trusts
in You. Trust in the Lord forever, for in Yah,
the Lord, is everlasting strength.

— Isaiah 26:3-4

GIVING *the* BEST *of* YOURSELF *to* YOUR SPOUSE

DAY 18

Waiting with Expectation

Waiting is never easy for anyone. But especially for those who are impatient, this is difficult. But when God has given us a promise, not only does He want us to wait, but to wait with expectation—knowing, believing, looking for that blessing, promises to manifest itself at any time in our life.

What does it mean to wait with expectation? Waiting with expectation means we are looking for our blessing, which we requested from God. It also means believing and knowing that God will do exactly what He promised.

> I will stand my watch
> And set myself on the rampart,
> And watch to see what He will say to me,
> And what I will answer when I am corrected.
> — Habakkuk 2:1

Think about it, what sense does it make to be waiting on something from God and not do so with the spirit of expectation. James 1:6–7 says a man who doubts should not expect to receive anything from God. So, if you're not waiting with an exception on your blessing, then you're doubting that your God will bring it to pass.

While waiting, be strong, do not doubt, do not waiver, just trust God.

> But let him ask in faith, with no doubting, for he who doubts is like a wave of the sea driven and tossed by the wind. For let not that man suppose that he will receive anything from the Lord; he is a double-minded man, unstable in all his ways.
>
> —James 1:6–8

> Wait on the Lord;
> Be of good courage,
> And He shall strengthen your heart;
> Wait, I say, on the Lord!
>
> — Psalm 27:14

God will also strengthen us while we exceptionally wait on His blessing. He said that

> But those who wait on the Lord shall renew their strength; They shall run and not be weary, They shall walk and not faint.
>
> — Isaiah 40:31

Expectation is our action motivated and activated by our faith in God. Faith without works is dead; faith without expectation is dead.

> Thus also faith by itself, if it does not have works, is dead.

You see then that a man is justified by
works, and not by faith only.

Likewise, was not Rahab the harlot also
justified by works when she received the mes-
sengers and sent them out another way?

For as the body without the spirit is dead,
so faith without works is dead also.

— James 2:17, 24–26

Faith and expectation work together as a team. *Faith* says
I believe God will do what I ask, even though I cannot see
it right now. *Expectation* says I am looking for what God has
promised to come to pass even though I don't have it yet.

Now faith is the substance of things hoped for,
the evidence of things not seen.

— Hebrews 11:1

For we walk by faith, not by sight.

— 2 Corinthians 5:7

The Bible is full of people who had faith. But they did
not just sit around and do nothing. No, they mixed their
faith with action. They had expectations, prayed, fasted, offered praises to their God, and they made confessions daily,
all on credit!

By faith Abel offered to God a more excellent
sacrifice than Cain, through which he obtained
witness that he was righteous, God testify-

ing of his gifts; and through it he being dead still speaks.

By faith Noah, being divinely warned of things not yet seen, moved with godly fear, prepared an ark for the saving of his household, by which he condemned the world and became heir of the righteousness which is according to faith.

Faithful Abraham

By faith Abraham obeyed when he was called to go out to the place which he would receive as an inheritance. And he went out, not knowing where he was going. By faith he dwelt in the land of promise as in a foreign country, dwelling in tents with Isaac and Jacob, the heirs with him of the same promise; for he waited for the city which has foundations, whose builder and maker is God.

By faith Sarah herself also received strength to conceive seed, and she bore a child when she was past the age, because she judged Him faithful who had promised. Therefore from one man, and him as good as dead, were born as many as the stars of the sky in multitude—innumerable as the sand which is by the seashore.

— Hebrews 11:4, 7–11

Waiting with expectation is waiting in faith!

GIVING *the* BEST *of* YOURSELF *to* YOUR SPOUSE

DAY 19

The Grace of God

Grace: favor, goodwill, generosity,
love, and protection—to honor or
favor, gratitude, benefits given.[16]
Most importantly, grace is
the favor of God.

Grace was given to us by God Himself when we did not
even deserve it and still do not deserve it now. Daily,
God surrounds us with His favor. Psalm 5:12 tells us that the
favor of God surrounds us like a shield. Now, if you think
about a shield, it protects just the front part of your body.
But the shield of God's favor surrounds our whole body and
protects us.

The favor of God is not automatic. It is not for everyone,
only the believers, God's children. You see, we receive the
grace of God when we accept Him into our hearts. We are
saved by grace first through faith. It is nothing that we can
take credit for.

For by grace are ye saved through faith; and
that not of yourselves: it is the gift of God:

---

[16] "Grace," The Free Dictionary Online (2021), https://www.thefreedictionary.com/grâce.
Ephesians 2:8-9

Not of works, lest any man should boast.
                                    — Ephesians 2:8–9

God extended this grace to us through the death of His son Jesus, our elder brother.

This grace is not to be missed, used, or taken for granted. The same grace that God extends to us we must extend to others as well. We must live a life pleasing to God, doing what He has told us to do. When we see our fellow brothers and sisters in Christ making mistakes instead of judging them, remember that if it were not for the grace that was extended to you, you would still be living in your sins, making the same mistake they just made. So, extend the hand of grace, the grace of God showing love, and understand and pray for them to be overcomers.

> But by the grace of God I am what I am, and
> His grace toward me was not in vain; but I la-
> bored more abundantly than they all, yet not I,
> but the grace of God which was with me.
>   — 1 Corinthians 15:10

> We then, as workers together with Him also
> plead with you not to receive the grace of
> God in vain. For He says: "In an acceptable
> time I have heard you, And in the day of sal-
> vation I have helped you." Behold, now is the
> accepted time; behold, now is the day of salva-
> tion.
>   — 2 Corinthians 6:1–2

GIVING *the* BEST *of* YOURSELF *to* YOUR SPOUSE

DAY 20

Showing the Love of God

Love: to be compassionate—to be a
friend, have affection.
An inner quality expressed outwardly
as a commitment to seek the well-
being of the other through concrete
acts of service.[17,18]

As you can see, there are many definitions for the word *love*, from acts of service to friendship. The greatest definitions of love can be found in the Bible. One of the biblical definitions of love states:

> "Love is patient, love is kind. It does not envy,
> it does not boast, it is not proud. It does not
> dishonor others, it is not self-seeking, it is not
> easily angered, it keeps no record of wrongs.
> Love does not delight in evil but rejoices with
> the truth."
>
> — 1 Corinthians 13:4–6 NIV

---

[17] Strong, *The New Strong's Complete Dictionary of Bible Words,* 157–158.
[18] David Noel Freedman, "Love," In *Eerdmans Dictionary of the Bible,* (Eerdmans; Edition Unstated, 2000), 825.

This is what love is. It protects always, trust always, hopes always, and preserves always. Love never fails.

> Love suffers long and is kind; love does not envy; love does not parade itself, is not puffed up; does not behave rudely, does not seek its own, is not provoked, thinks no evil; does not rejoice in iniquity, but rejoices in the truth; bears all things, believes all things, hopes all things, endures all things.
>
> Love never fails. But whether there are prophecies, they will fail; whether there are tongues, they will cease; whether there is knowledge, it will vanish away. For we know in part and we prophesy in part. But when that which is perfect has come, then that which is in part will be done away.
>
> When I was a child, I spoke as a child, I understood as a child, I thought as a child; but when I became a man, I put away childish things. For now we see in a mirror, dimly, but then face to face. Now I know in part, but then I shall know just as I also am known.
>
> And now abide faith, hope, love, these three; but the greatest of these is love.
>
> — 1 Corinthians 13:4–13

Another great definition of love is Jesus. He showed us His love by surrendering His life on calvary's cross. This is while we were still lost in sin and wanted nothing to do with Him **(John 15:13)**.

How do we know that the love of Christ is in us? We do so by walking in His character, the fruits of the spirit.

> But the fruit of the Spirit is love, joy, peace, longsuffering, kindness, goodness, faithfulness, gentleness, self-control. Against such there is no law.
>
> — Galatians 5:22–23

When we show the love of God to those around us, we are showing them God Himself.

> You shall not take vengeance, nor bear any grudge against the children of your people, but you shall love your neighbor as yourself: I am the Lord.
>
> — Leviticus 19:18

> For all the law is fulfilled in one word, even in this: "You shall love your neighbor as yourself."
>
> — Galatians 5:14

> And the second is like it: 'You shall love your neighbor as yourself.'
>
> — Matthew 22:39

Love covers a multitude of sins.

And above all things have fervent love
for one another, for "love will cover a multitude of sins."

— I Peter 4:8

When we love people without passing judgments, we are showing the love of God.

_____

_____

_____

_____

_____

_____

_____

_____

_____

_____

_____

_____

_____

_____

_____

DAY 21

Fueling the Passion of God in Our Lives

What drives your relationship with the Lord? Is it knowing that He is faithful, loving, caring, and a God that is worthy to be worshipped? For us, it is all the above and then some.

The definition of the word **fuel** is food.[19] Anything burned to produce energy or heat.

Passion is defined as a "strong and barely controllable emotion."[20]

When putting both words together, we can say we need Jesus for spiritual food, which comes from His Word. We need to serve Him with strong emotion, with our whole heart.

There are times in our Christian journey that we get comfortable in whom we have become or what we have done through the help of God. But God does not want us to become complacent. Instead, He always wants us to fuel our passion and the hunger we have for Him daily, like the first day we gave our life to Him.

---

[19] "Fuel" (Cambridge Learner's Online Dictionary, 2021), https://dictionary.cambridge.org/us/dictionary/learner-english/fuel.

[20] "Passion," (Oxford Online Dictionary. Lexico. Com., 2021), https://www.lexico.com/en/definition/passion.

Therefore I remind you to stir up the gift of God which is in you through the laying on of my hands.

— 2 Timothy 1:6

But He answered and said, "It is written, 'Man shall not live by bread alone, but by every word that proceeds from the mouth of God.'"

— Matthew 4:4

There are times on our faith journey that we become dry and thirsty and need to be watered like plants. God calls us to come by and drink at no cost to us; run to Him for a refresher.

"Ho! Everyone who thirsts,
Come to the waters;
And you who have no money,
Come, buy and eat.
Yes, come, buy wine and milk
Without money and without price.
Why do you spend money for what is not bread,
And your wages for what does not satisfy?
Listen carefully to Me, and eat what is good,
And let your soul delight itself in abundance.
Incline your ear, and come to Me.
Hear, and your soul shall live;
And I will make an everlasting covenant with you—
The sure mercies of David.

— Isaiah 55:1–3

He will always fill us when we hunger and thirst for Him.

We must allow God to stir up the gifts of the Holy Spirit that lives within us—allowing those gifts to pour out and bring life to us and others.

> Jesus answered and said to her, "Whoever
> drinks of this water will thirst again, "but who-
> ever drinks of the water that I shall give him
> will never thirst. But the water that I shall give
> him will become in him a fountain of water
> springing up into everlasting life."
> —John 4:13–14

> On the last day, that great day of the feast, Jesus
> stood and cried out, saying, "If anyone thirsts,
> let him come to Me and drink. He who believes
> in Me, as the Scripture has said, out of his
> heart will flow rivers of living water."
> —John 7:37–38

We cannot expect to live a godly life full of passion for God without being partakers of His Word.

> But He answered and said, "It is written, 'Man
> shall not live by bread alone, but by every word
> that proceeds from the mouth of God.'"
> — Matthew 4:4

GIVING *the* BEST *of* YOURSELF *to* YOUR SPOUSE

DAY 22

The Virtuous Marriage

Virtuous: moral excellence and righteousness.[21]

Is there such a thing as a virtuous marriage, and if there is, what is the appearance of one?

Let us start with what a virtuous marriage is not. A virtuous marriage is not a selfish marriage, where one spouse just thinks of him or herself all the time, as well as their personal needs. In a virtuous marriage, there is no getting your way all the time. A virtuous marriage is not one-sided. Scripture tells us in Ephesians 5:31 that a man leaves his mother and father and is joined to his wife, and the two become one flesh. They are no longer separate but one flesh. Though they have their own identities, they no longer belong to themselves but to each other. We see this same analogy in the creation of woman.

> So the LORD God caused the man to fall into a
> deep sleep; and while he was sleeping, he took
> one of the man's ribs and then closed up the
> place with flesh.

---

[21] "Virtuous," Merriam-Webster Online Dictionary (Merriam-Webster, Incorporated, 2021), https://www.merriam-webster.com/dictionary/virtuous.

Then the LORD God made a woman from the rib he had taken out of the man, and he brought her to the man.

The man said, "This is now bone of my bones and flesh of my flesh; she shall be called 'woman,' for she was taken out of man."

That is why a man leaves his father and mother and is united to his wife, and they become one flesh.

— Genesis 2:21–24

A virtuous marriage is a husband and wife working together as one. Does this mean they always agree? No, but they work together as one; they do not undermine each other. A virtuous marriage is a supporting and healthy marriage. Husbands and wives love each other. They encourage each other. Husband and wife pray together and for each other, they attend fellowship together, they study the Word of God together. In a virtuous marriage, they both share the responsibilities of the home. But the wife recognizes the husband as the head of the home. A virtuous marriage is a healthy marriage where God is the center.

_____

_____

_____

_____

_____

DAY 23

His Needs

When God created Adam, he was alone in creation. So, God created the animals, but Adam did not find fulfillment in the animals God had created–the fulfillment that man needs from another humankind. God then created women from the rib of Adam. God called this woman Eve.

> And the LORD God said, "It is not good that man should be alone; I will make him a helper comparable to him." Out of the ground the LORD God formed every beast of the field and every bird of the air, and brought them to Adam to see what he would call them. And whatever Adam called each living creature, that was its name. So Adam gave names to all cattle, to the birds of the air, and to every beast of the field. But for Adam there was not found a helper comparable to him. And the LORD God caused a deep sleep to fall on Adam, and he slept; and He took one of his ribs, and closed up the flesh in its place. Then the rib which the LORD God had taken from man He

made into a woman, and He brought her to the man.

— Genesis 2:18–22

So, what does a man need to feel fulfilled? Melanie Chitwood, in her book *What a Husband Needs from His Wife*, talks about a helper. A husband needs a helper. This is part of why he gets married.[22] She also says that a helper is a companion.[23] Eve was Adam's companion; a companion is also a friend. Chitwood says, "A helper who is a companion helps meet her husband's needs for friendship."[24] That is great. It is particularly important that a husband and wife are friends, as matter of fact, they should be each other's best friend. Even if you did not start out that way, you could become best friends. Chitwood goes on to say, "A friend has to listen to her husband without interrupting or judging."[25] She says a friend notices everything about her husband, including when he has had a long day at the office.[26] A friend goes the distance for their husband, doing the little things, a friend makes time for her husband. All these are great qualities of a friend and how a marriage should look.

Scripture tells us that a friend sticks closer than a brother.

A man who has friends must himself be friendly, But there is a friend who sticks closer than a brother.

— Proverbs 18:24

---

[22] Chitwood, Melanie. 2006. *What a Husband Needs from His Wife*. Eugene, OR: Harvest House Publishers.

[23] Ibid.

[24] Ibid.

[25] Chitwood, *What a Husband Needs from His*. Eugene, 2006.

[26] Ibid.

A husband and wife must stick close to each other, have each other's backs. Therefore a man leaves his mother and father, and what? Cleaves to his wife, and the two become one flesh, no longer two but one.

> "For this reason a man shall leave his father
> and mother and be joined to his wife, and the
> two shall become one flesh."
> — Ephesians 5:31

What is one of the things a man needs from his wife? A helper, a companion, and a friend. These three characteristics work together as one.

✀

_____

_____

_____

_____

_____

_____

_____

_____

_____

DAY 24

Her Needs

When God created women from the rib of the first man, He created her to be the helper for the man. But have you ever stopped to ask or wonder what about the woman's needs? Yes, a woman was created from the man and is to be his helper and respect him. But just as a man needs respect, so does a woman. A woman needs to know that her husband loves and respects her. A woman needs to feel needed. A woman needs to feel appreciated by her man. Too often in marriages, we get focused on the husband's needs and neglect the needs of the wife. But for the marriage to be one accord, both the husband and the wife need to work together.

> Submit to one another out of reverence for Christ.
>
> — Ephesians 5:21 NIV

Scripture tells us that a man "who finds a wife finds what is good and receives favor from the Lord" (Proverbs 18:22 NIV). Husbands are to love their wives as Christ loves the Church and gave his life for her and made her holy.

Husbands, love your wives, just as Christ also
loved the church and gave Himself for her,
that He might sanctify and cleanse her with the
washing of water by the word,

— Ephesians 5:25–26

A woman needs holiness through and from her husband.
The husband is to love his wife as he loves himself.

For no one ever hated his own flesh, but nour-
ishes and cherishes it, just as the Lord does the
church.

— Ephesians 5:29

When the needs of the husband and the wife are met mu-
tually, this makes for a long-lasting marriage and a peaceful
home for everyone.

☙

_____

_____

_____

_____

_____

_____

_____

_____

DAY 25

What Makes a Man Feel Loved?

When you sit back and think about it, what makes your man feel loved? Sometimes all it takes are the little things. As I think about the little things that make my husband feel loved is by me spending time with him watching a sporting event on tv or a movie. To him, that means a lot. It means that I am taking time out for him. We often take these little things for granted in the busyness of life. But it is the little things that count the most. Scripture tells us that a little leaven destroys the whole lump.

> A little leaven leavens the whole lump.
> — Galatians 5:9

In the same way, in a marriage, it's the little things that we don't do that destroy our marriages.

Sex is an especially important part of marriage unity. This should be tops for both husband and wife, but often the husband is the aggressor in the bedroom. Tell the truth and shame the devil. Does it seem as if that is all men think about, Ladies?

A man feels loved when he is respected by his wife. The man is the head of the house, as God is the head of the Church.

Wives, submit to your own husbands, as to the Lord.

For the husband is head of the wife, as also Christ is head of the church; and He is the Savior of the body.

Therefore, just as the church is subject to Christ, so let the wives be to their own husbands in everything.

— Ephesians 5:22–24

He not only needs to feel respected but also needs to feel supported when it comes to the matters of the home. He wants to know that when he feels like giving up, you are there for him, that you have his back.

Marriage is hard work, but it can work when you work together as a team, holding each other up. Supporting each other, but especially the man of the house. They do not ever want to feel like they are failures, but they do want to feel loved!

_____

_____

_____

_____

_____

_____

DAY 26

What Makes a Woman Feel Loved?

God created marriage for men and women to have a mate for life. Marriage is not only a covenant between the man and woman but also between God. We promise to be faithful to another before God. What does a woman want in her marriage? What makes her feel loved? Faithfulness, respect, appreciation, and gifts do not hurt every once in a while.

Personally, I love flowers. It does not hurt to give a girl some gifts to say, "Honey... I love and appreciate you for taking care of the home, working a full-time job, and taking care of the kids and me." Women, can I get an amen!

Scripture tells us that love covers a multitude of sins.

> And above all things have fervent love for one
> another, for "love will cover a multitude of
> sins."
> — I Peter 4:8

When in mutual love in a marital relationship, it covers both spouses. When we have wronged each other, that same love should allow us to forgive each other, correct each other in that same manner of love. The songwriter Travis Green says God's love is a banner over us, over our lives. His love covers us.

> Oh, if you forget, just lift your head
> My banner over you is love[27]

Just as a man never wants to feel like he is a failure, a woman never wants to feel like she is not a good wife or mother to her children. She always wants to know that she is the soul of the family unit, the helpmate of her husband, taken from Adam's rib.

> And the Lord God caused a deep sleep to fall on Adam, and he slept; and He took one of his ribs, and closed up the flesh in its place.
> Then the rib which the Lord God had taken from man He made into a woman, and He brought her to the man.
>
> — Genesis 2:21–22

---

[27] "Travis Greene - Good & Loved Lyrics" (Azlyrics.Com., 2021), https://www.azlyrics.com/lyrics/travisgreene/goodloved.html.

DAY 27

Intimacy

Intimacy: the state of being intimate; familiarity.[28]

What is intimacy in a marriage? I have heard it said that when you look closely at the word intimacy, this is what you see... *In-to-me-see*. This makes a lot of sense when you think about when you are intimate with your spouse, you're not just looking at the outer person but a personal inner relationship.

In marital intimacy, a husband and wife share a piece of each other with their spouse. We see each other's soul for the good or bad that it may be. Intimacy is more than sex in a marital relationship. Intimacy is spending quality time together, laughing together. Intimacy is also communicating regularly with each other such as date nights, etc. No silent treatment, guys. All these make for intimacy in a marriage. An intimate marriage is a good marriage, not saying that there won't be difficulties, but when you work together, you can get through the difficulties together.

It is said that:

---

[28] "Intimate," Merriam-Webster Online Dictionary (Merriam-Webster, Incorporated, 2021), https://www.merriam-webster.com/dictionary/intimate.

Intimacy is closeness between people in personal relationships. It is what builds over time as you connect with someone, grow to care about each other, and feel more and more comfortable during your time together. It can include physical or emotional closeness, or even a mix of the two.[29]

Dr. Douglas Weiss, in his book *Intimacy: A 100-Day Guide To Lasting Relationships*, says intimacy is not a mystery; it is a process.[30] In other words, you have to take steps to build an intimate relationship with your spouse, i.e., some of the things mentioned before, date nights, healthy communications, etc. Intimacy is a beautiful thing when we make it a priority in our marriage.

---

[29] Maisha Johnson, "Intimacy: 32 Things to Know About Friendships, Relationships, More" (Healthline Media, 2019), https://www.healthline.com/health/intimacy#overview.
[30] Douglas Weiss, *Intimacy: A 100-Day Guide to Lasting Relationships* (Lake Mary, FL: Siloam Charisma Media/Charisma House Book Group, 2003).

DAY 28

What Causes a Breakdown of Intimacy?

W hat causes a breakdown or a lack of intimacy in a marriage? According to Dr. Weiss, one of the things that cause the breakdown of intimacy in a marriage is a couple's sins and unresolved conflicts with each other during their marriage.[31] These unresolved conflicts or issues open the door to other emotions such as anger, disappointment, neglect of each other, and a lack of communication. At this point, couples may refuse to share what is on their hearts or minds with each other. They may even become afraid of what the other spouse may say or do because of this breakdown in intimacy.

Remember we said that intimacy is *in-to-me-see*. So, when that is broken down, we are not allowing the other person to see our hearts, the hurts, the pain, the distrust. Sometimes all they see is the byproduct of the lack of that intimacy, which is mostly anger. Ephesians 4:25–26 tells us to do not let the sun go down on our anger and do not sin because of our anger.

You see, anger can cause us to sin against each other. We do things we regret doing after it's done. Anger is a real emotion, but we cannot get caught up in it because it can destroy us and our marriages, especially the intimacy that God

---

[31] Douglas, *Intimacy: A 100-Day Guide to Lasting Relationships.*

proposed to be a part of marriage. Scripture also tells us to be angry and sin not.

> Be angry, and do not sin.
>
> — Psalm 4:4a

We can be angry at our spouse and not sin. We can answer with kind words. We can speak in kind words and tones even if the other words are not so kind. Scripture tells us not to repay evil for evil "but overcome evil with good" (Romans 12:21 KJV). I like to say it this way, overcome evil with love. Love and forgiveness bring healing to any situation, and they can do the same for intimacy breakdown in our marriages. Love covers a multitude of sins.

> Hatred stirs up strife, But love covers all sins.
>
> — Proverbs 10:12

DAY 29

How Do We Make Intimacy a Part of Our Daily Lives?

How do we make intimacy a part of our daily lives as married couples? Everything happens one day at a time; intimacy is no different. To develop intimacy in our marriages, we must go at it one day at a time. We must make an effort every day to spend time with our spouses, to go on lunch dates, breakfast dates, date nights, etc. Every little bit helps; we make time for everything else in our lives, we should take time for each other.

I remember when my husband and I were dating, I lived in New Jersey, and he was living in the windy city/Chicago. We would be on the phone for hours talking, and mind you, I did not have a house phone as I lived in an apartment, so I was out in the cold on a payphone with him. Mind you, I was calling him collect too. The things we do in the beginning, we neglect to do them when we get married. Dr. Weiss says, "Passion is a dividend of consistent investment made into a relationship."[32] In other words, what you put in is what you get out, what you put into or the lack thereof making intimacy possible in your marriage is what you will get out.

Little things mean a lot in a marriage and create much intimacy. Saying thank you to your spouse for doing the

[32] Douglas, *Intimacy: A 100-Day Guide to Lasting Relationships*.

laundry, taking out the garbage. That makes for some great reward after the kids are down for the night. Little things stir on intimacy in a marriage. Let us not let our schedules and daily routines get in the way of experiencing the intimacy God intended for us to have in our marriages. Please take advantage of the little things, remember what it was like to date or court your wife.

My husband and I did not start doing date nights or dates until about six years ago, and we have been going on twenty-six years of marriage. He did not think he had to date his wife; his thoughts were, *I already got her, why do I need to date her?* But you see, this part of how you keep the marriage bed fresh and the intimacy going. We make an effort to go on a date at least twice a month. It is not always going out of the house. Sometimes it is an intimate dinner at home, a movie night, or a day just enjoying each other's company. We must work at creating daily intimacy in our marriages.

DAY 30

A Marriage Made on the Earth

We often hear this phrase, but what does it really mean? What is a marriage made on the earth? What does that look like in reality? Glad you asked those questions. First, it's one made with the covenant of love. Love is the foundation of our Christian faith, and as Christian married couples, it should also be the foundation of our marriage. People nowadays marry for all kinds of different reasons. Some marry for money; others marry for prestige, fame, and so on. But the B tells us that this should not be so. God created marriage to be a covenant relationship between a man and a woman, not for anything else.

A marriage made on the earth is where God is at the head of each of our lives, and therefore the head of the marriage. We put God first in our marriage, decision-making, and planning. We realize that we are nothing without Him and that our marriage cannot work without Him in it.

A marriage made on the earth is where the husband and wife honor their marriage vows to each other. You know the parts we like to forget when we get mad at each other... For richer, for poor, in sickness and in health, until death do us part. You see, divorce was never part of God's plan for marriage. Mark 10:9 says what God has joined together, let no man take apart.

A marriage made on the earth is not necessarily one without troubles, but it is one that will continue to honor the marriage vows even in the midst of those troubles, the one that will continue to love in spite of. This is what a marriage made on the earth is and should look like for the Bible-believing, Bible-reading Christians!

As we continue to work and improve our marriage, we pray that this encourages each couple that goes through this devotional. It is our prayer that you were inspired and encouraged by this devotional. We thank each of you for taking time out of your busy schedule to work on and improve your marriage. Continue to study and implement things that will improve your marriage. May God continue to bless you and your marriage.

— Nigel and Anrick Smith

REFERENCES

Chitwood, Melanie. 2006. *What a Husband Needs from His*. Eugene, OR: Harvest House Publishers.

"Compassion." 2016. In *Merriam-Webster Intermediate Dictionary*, 154. Springfield, MA: Merriam-Webster Incorporated.

"Faith." 2021. Merriam-Webster Online Dictionary. Merriam-Webster, Incorporated. 2021. https://www.merriam-webster.com/dictionary/faith.

Freedman, David Noel, Ed. 2000. "Prayer." In *Eerdmans Dictionary of the Bible*. Grand Rapids, MI: William B. Eerdmans Publishing Company.

Freedman, David Noel. 2000. "Love." In *Eerdmans Dictionary of the Bible*, 825. Eerdmans; Edition Unstated.

"Fuel." 2021. Cambridge Learner's Online Dictionary. 2021. https://dictionary.cambridge.org/us/dictionary/learner-english/fuel.

"Grâce." 2021. The Free Dictionary Online. 2021. https://www.thefreedictionary.com/grâce.

"Intimate." 2021. Merriam-Webster Online Dictionary. Merriam-Webster, Incorporated. 2021. https://www.merriam-webster.com/dictionary/intimate.

Johnson, Maisha. 2019. "Intimacy: 32 Things to Know About Friendships, Relationships, More."

Healthline Media. 2019. https://www.healthline.com/health/intimacy#overview.

"Joyce Meyer Ministries - Enjoying Everyday Life TV Show." 2021. Joyce Meyer Ministries. 2021. https://joycemeyer.org/todaysshow.

"Know." 2016. In *Merriam-Webster Intermediate Dictionary*, 433. Springfield, MA: Merriam-Webster Incorporated.

"Love: NCCG.ORG." 2018. The Messianic Evangelicals. 2018. http://nccg.org/love.html.

Omartian, Stormie. 2014. *The Power of a Praying Wife*. Eugene, OR: Harvest House Publishers.

"Passion." 2021. Oxford Online Dictionary. Lexico. Com. 2021. https://www.lexico.com/en/definition/passion.

"Quote by Anonymous." 2021. Quotespedia. 2021. https://www.quotespedia.org/authors/a/anonymous/keep-going-everything-you-need-will-come-to-you-at-the-perfect-time-anonymous/.

"Restoration." 2016. In *Merriam-Webster Intermediate Dictionary*, 674. Springfield, MA: Merriam-Webster Incorporated.

Soukhanov, Anne H., Kaethe Ellis, Laurel Cook, and Howard Webber. 1988a. "Prayer." In *Webster's II New Riverside University Dictionary*, 616. Boston, MA: Riverside Publishing Co.

———. 1988b. "Virtuous." In *Webster's II New Riverside University Dictionary*, 282. Boston, MA: Riverside Publishing Co.

"Steward." 2016. In *Merriam-Webster Intermediate Dictionary*, 787. Springfield, MA: Merriam-Webster Incorporated.

Strong, James. 1996. *The New Strong's Complete Dictionary of Bible Words*. Nelsonword Publishing Group.

"Sustain." 2021. Merriam-Webster Online Dictionary. Merriam-Webster, Incorporated. 2021. https://www.merriam-webster.com/dictionary/sustain.

The Holy Bible: King James Version [KJV]. 1999. New York, NY: American Bible Society. Public Domain.

The Holy Bible: New American Standard Bible [NASB]. 1995. The Lockman Foundation. http://www.lockman.org/nasb/index.php.

The Holy Bible: New International Version [NIV]. 1984. Grand Rapids: Zonderman Publishing House. https://www.biblegateway.com/versions/New-International-Version-NIV-Bible/#booklist.

The Holy Bible: The New King James Version [NKJV]. 1999. Nashville, TN: Thomas Nelson, Inc. https://www.biblegateway.com/versions/New-King-James-Version-NKJV-Bible/#booklist.

"Travis Greene - Good & Loved Lyrics." 2021. Azlyrics. Com. 2021. https://www.azlyrics.com/lyrics/travisgreene/goodloved.html.

"Trust." 2016. In *Merriam-Webster Intermediate Dictionary*, 863. Springfield, MA: Merriam-Webster Incorporated.

"Virtuous." 2021. Merriam-Webster Online Dictionary. Merriam-Webster, Incorporated. 2021. https://www.merriam-webster.com/dictionary/virtuous.

Weiss, Douglas. 2003. *Intimacy: A 100-Day Guide to Lasting Relationships*. Lake Mary, FL: Siloam Charisma Media/Charisma House Book Group.

ABOUT THE AUTHORS

Nigel and Anrick are both veterans of the United States Army, where they met and were married. They have been married for over twenty years and have two children Michael and Alexandria. Nigel holds a bachelor's degree from Trident University in Business Administration, and Anrick holds an associate of arts in Interdisciplinary Studies and a bachelor's in Early Childhood Education from Liberty University. They are both leaders in the community and elders in their home church New Birth Outreach Church in Columbus, Georgia. They both make Phenix City, Alabama, their home.